EARLIER AMERICAN MUSIC
EDITED BY H. WILEY HITCHCOCK
for the *Music Library Association*

24

ARTHUR FOOTE

SUITE IN E MAJOR
Opus 63

AND

SERENADE IN E MAJOR
Opus 25

ARTHUR FOOTE

SUITE IN E MAJOR
Opus 63

AND

SERENADE IN E MAJOR
Opus 25

New Introduction by H. Wiley Hitchcock

DA CAPO PRESS • NEW YORK • 1983

EDITOR'S FOREWORD

American musical culture, from Colonial and Federal Era days on, has been reflected in an astonishing production of printed music of all kinds: by 1820, for instance, more than fifteen thousand musical publications had issued from American presses. Fads, fashions, and tastes have changed so rapidly in our history, however, that comparatively little earlier American music has remained in print. On the other hand, the past few decades have seen an explosion of interest in earlier American culture, including earlier American music. College and university courses in American civilization and American music have proliferated; recording companies have found a surprising response to earlier American composers and their music; a wave of interest in folk and popular music of past eras has opened up byways of musical experience unimagined only a short time ago.

It seems an opportune moment, therefore, to make available for study and enjoyment — and as an aid to furthering performance of earlier American music — works of significance that exist today only in a few scattered copies of publications long out of print, and works that may be well known only in later editions or arrangements having little relationship to the original compositions.

Earlier American Music is planned around several types of musical scores to be reprinted from early editions of the eighteenth, nineteenth, and early twentieth centuries. The categories are as follows:

> Songs and other solo vocal music
> Choral music and part-songs
> Solo keyboard music
> Chamber music
> Orchestral music and concertos
> Dance music and marches for band
> Theater music

The idea of *Earlier American Music* originated in a paper read before the Music Library Association in February, 1968, and published under the title "A Monumenta Americana?" in the Association's journal, *Notes* (September, 1968). It seems most appropriate, therefore, for the Music Library Association to sponsor this series. We hope *Earlier American Music* will stimulate further study and performance of musical Americana.

H. Wiley Hitchcock

INTRODUCTION

In the third quarter of the nineteenth century, there were born in New England about a dozen men, and one woman, who were to become our first significant composers of large-scale concert music: George Chadwick (born 1854), Arthur Whiting (1861), Horatio Parker (1863), Amy Cheney Beach (1867), Henry F. Gilbert (1868), Henry Hadley and Frederick Converse (both 1871), Edward Burlingame Hill (1872), and Daniel Gregory Mason (1873). (Charles Ives, born in 1874, and Carl Ruggles, born in 1876, were not to be recognized as "significant" until much, much later than these others.) Another of this "Second New England School" of American composers (as it has been called), slightly older than any of those just cited, was Arthur Foote.

Foote was born in Salem, Massachuetts, on March 1853. As a boy he had piano lessons and studied harmony at the recently founded New England Conservatory in Boston. He entered Harvard University in 1870; there he had music courses with John Knowles Paine, senior citizen of America's developing concert-music community (but still a few years away from being officially named a professor of music—the first American academic to be given that title).

Foote had no intention of becoming a professional musician; he thought he would probably enter Harvard Law School, but, as he wrote in his autobiography (1927; printed 1946; reprinted 1978), "fate stepped in and the profession of law escaped one rather inefficient exponent." "Fate" took the form of urgings by Benjamin Johnson Lang, with whom Foote had organ and piano lessons during the summer following his graduation from Harvard, that he embark on a musical career. So, back to Harvard and further study with Paine went Foote, and in June 1875 he was awarded a Master of Arts degree—the first such degree for concentration in music to be awarded by an American university; his thesis was on "The [Historical] Development of the Secular Style in [Vocal] Music." (Lacking the qualifying adjectives, Foote's title is a bit vague.)

That summer he opened a studio in Salem, moving it to Boston in December, to begin a long career as a teacher of piano, organ, and composition. He also became organist of the First Church (Unitarian) of Boston, where he served for thirty-two years (1878–1910); and from 1920 to 1937 (when he contracted a fatal case of pneumonia) he taught piano at the New England Conservatory.

Foote was very lucky, for an American composer of his time, in both performance and publication opportunities for his music. The Boston Symphony Orchestra, founded in 1881, introduced most of his orchestra works, and he was championed by the most celebrated string quartet in the thirty years before World War I, the Kneisel Quartet (to the members of which Foote dedicated, "in Freundschaft," his *Piano Quintet,* op. 38). Also, beginning with his Opus 1 *(Drei Stücke für Pianoforte und Violoncell),* virtually everything Foote wrote was printed by the Boston music publisher Arthur P. Schmidt, who in gratitude for an American career (he was German-born) made it a matter of conscience to publish works by Americans.

For a composer as long-lived as Foote, his catalogue is not impressively large: excluding arrangements of his own works, there are about 200 compositions, more than half of them songs and small choral pieces, written over a span of forty-five years from 1877 to 1922.* Until about 1910, he titled most of his instrumental works in German (e.g. the *Drei Stücke,* op. 1, cited above); this reflected faithfully the musical orientation of Boston at the time (at least as far as concert music was concerned)—one of unabashed adulation for the Austro-Germanic style of the Classic/Romantic era. (Foote was in fact unique, as a member of the Second New England School or the "Boston Group," as it has also been called, in not having hied himself off to Leipzig or Munich or Vienna to perfect his craft as a composer. On the other hand, in the first twenty years of his professional career he made no fewer than eight trips to Europe.)

Foote seems to have found composing for stringed instruments, in various combinations, particularly congenial. All his chamber works, except the *Trois Pièces,* op. 31, for oboe and piano, include strings, and works for string orchestra predominate among his pieces for large ensembles. Besides the two compositions included in the present volume, there are other attractive string-orchestra works, such as *An Irish Folk Song,* arranged by Foote from his most popular song, and *A Night Piece* for flute and strings, arranged in 1922 from a *Nocturne* for flute and string quartet, and perhaps Foote's best-known work.

The *Serenade in E dur für Streich-Orchester,* as it is titled in the 1892 score published by Schmidt, was—like a number of Foote's larger works— a mélange of earlier compositions reworked and combined into a "final state." The first of his string-orchestra pieces had been a *Suite in E Major,* op. 12, composed in 1885–86 in three movements: Allegro comodo, Andante con moto, and Gavotte. In the summer of 1889, on Nantucket Island, Foote completed a *Suite No. 2 in D Major,* op. 21, for string orchestra; it had four movements—Prelude, Minuetto, Air, and Gavotte—and at its first performance (by the Boston Symphony Orchestra, on 22 November 1889) it was called "Serenade for String Orchestra, op. 21." Then, in 1891, Foote reworked the Air and Minuet of the latter work, together with the earlier three-movement suite, op. 12; re-titled some of the movements; and fashioned thereby the *Serenade in E Major,* op. 25. This he dedicated, as the title-page indicates, to Henry L. Higginson, the wealthy banker who had founded (and in the early years made up the deficits of) the Boston Symphony Orchestra. The *Serenade* seems to have had its premiere performance, surprisingly, not in Boston but in Baltimore, on 5 January 1893, on the program of the third concert of the fledgling Baltimore Orchestra, although the Boston Symphony under Arthur Nikisch performed it slightly later in the same season. Its five movements (two of which, the Air and the Romanze, may be omitted, we are informed on the first page of the score) represent Foote at his most graceful—serene, self-contained, a true member of that classicizing wing of post-Romanticism embodied most matchlessly in Brahms.

---

*For most of the details and dates that follow, I am indebted to Wilma Reid Cipolla, *A Catalog of the Works of Arthur Foote* (Detroit, 1980). Ms. Cipolla has also contributed a valuable introduction to the Da Capo Press reprint (1978) of Foote's *Autobiography.*

The *Suite in E dur für Streich-Orchester,* op. 63, rivals *A Night Piece* as Foote's most frequently performed work. Like the *Serenade* for strings, it too, as we find it in the score published in 1909 by Schmidt, is a work in "final state." Originally, as composed in 1907, it had as its second movement a Theme and Variations, and the other movements carried English titles—Prelude, Pizzicato and Adagietto, and Fugue; in 1908, Foote dropped the Theme and Variations (which was never published, although the manuscript survives). Here is Foote at his most elegant, craftsmanly, and—especially in the Pizzicato sub-movements—witty. The Praeludium is admirably economical in subject matter: everything flows from the theme of the opening measures. The "capricious" Pizzicato sections, flanking a lyrical Adagietto to make up the second movement, are inevitably reminiscent of the second movement of Tchaikovsky's Fourth Symphony (dating from 1877 and, be it remembered, still "modern" at the turn of the century, when Foote composed his suite); but there are hints of an "American hustle" and even a tiny tinge of rag-like syncopation that betray a birthplace in Boston rather than St. Petersburg. The final fugue is noble, thoroughly worked out, and satisfyingly capped by a remarkably resonant, skillfully prepared climax.

In sum, here are two important works—one justly well known, the other unjustly neglected—in a medium particularly favored by the composer, a major figure among the first group of American composers in the larger forms of concert music.

H. WILEY HITCHCOCK

SUITE IN E MAJOR

Opus 63

MAX FIEDLER
gewidmet.

SUITE
in E dur

(Praeludium-Pizzicato und Adagietto-Fuge)

FÜR

STREICH-ORCHESTER

VON

ARTHUR FOOTE
OP. 63.

Partitur......Pr. $\frac{M. 3.}{\$. 1.50}$ n.
Stimmen .....Pr. $\frac{M. 5.}{\$. 2.50}$

ARTHUR P. SCHMIDT
BOSTON   LEIPZIG   NEW YORK
120 Boylston St.   Lindenstrasse 16.   11 West 36 th St.

Suite in E dur.
I.
Praeludium.

Arthur Foote, Op. 63.

Allegro comodo. (♩ = 76-88)

a tempo

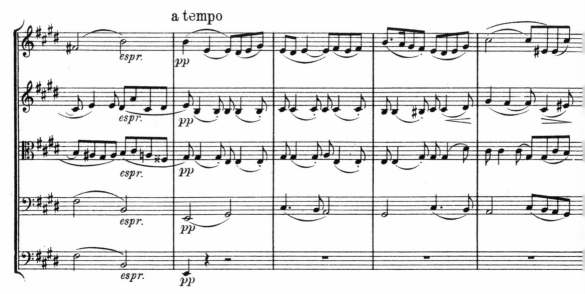

5

6

a tempo

a tempo

II.

Pizzicato und Adagietto.

Capriccioso. Allegretto. ($\downarrow$. $= 96$)

14

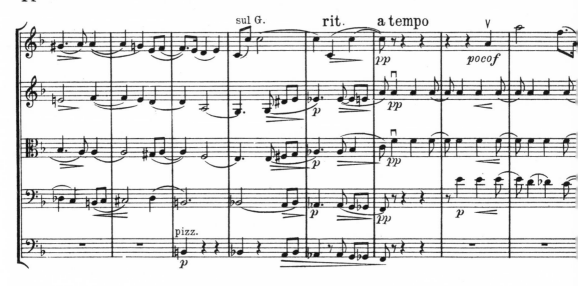

A.P.S. 8480

III.

Fuge.

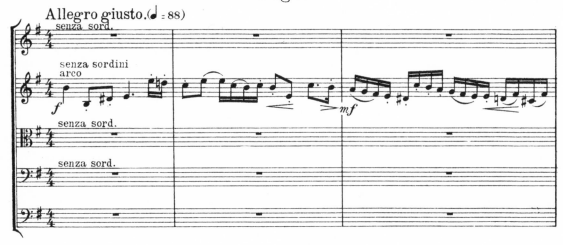

22

A.P.S.8480

26

Stich und Druck von C.G.Röder G.m.b.H., Leipzig

SERENADE IN E MAJOR

Opus 25

Herrn Henry L. Higginson gewidmet.

Serenade.

in E DUR
für Streich-Orchester

(Praeludium - Air - Intermezzo - Romanze - Gavotte)

von

ARTHUR FOOTE.

2810.

OP. 25.

$ 1 25
Mk 2 50

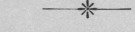

Eigenthum des Verlegers für alle Länder

BOSTON & LEIPZIG.

ARTHUR P. SCHMIDT.

SERENADE
in E-dur
für Streich-Orchester.

I. Praeludium.

ARTHUR FOOTE, OP. 25

N.B. Der zweite ("Air") oder vierte Satz ("Romanze") kann, wenn nothwendig, ausgelassen werden.

Copyright 1892 Arthur P. Schmidt.

Molto più Allegro.(♩ = 80.)

(= 88.)

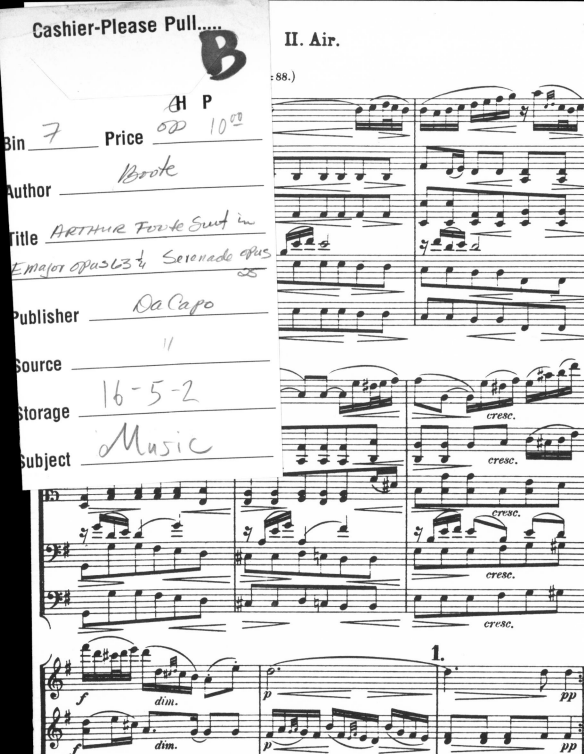

III. Intermezzo.

poco a poco - - rall. -

a tempo

3.

3.

a tempo
(Solo.)
(senza sordini)
rit.
rit.
rit.
rit.
rit.
pizz.
cresc.
6.
cresc.
arco
6.

IV. Romanze.

V. Gavotte.

Allegro deciso. (♩= 76.)

Più Allegro. ($\circ$ = 88.)

The Complete
EARLIER AMERICAN MUSIC SERIES

1 **John Knowles Paine**
SYMPHONY NO. 1 (Op. 23)
(Leipzig 1908)

2 **Horatio W. Parker**
HORA NOVISSIMA
The Rhythm of Bernard De Morlaix
on the Celestial Country
(London & New York, 1900)

3 **George W. Chadwick**
JUDITH
Lyric Drama For Soli, Chorus, and Orchestra
(New York, 1901)

4 **George W. Chadwick**
SYMPHONY NO. 2 in B Flat (Opus 21)
(Boston, 1888)

5 **Ira D. Sanky et al.**
GOSPEL HYMNS NOS. 1 to 6 Complete
(New York, 1895)

6 **Supply Belcher**
THE HARMONY OF MAINE
(Boston, 1794)

7 **Edward MacDowell**
SONGS (Op. 40, 47, 56, 58, 60) (1890-1902)

8 **Edward MacDowell**
PIANO PIECES (Op. 51, 55, 61, 62) (1869-1902)

9 **THE AMERICAN MUSIC MISCELLANY**
A Collection of the Newest and Most
Approved Songs, Set to Music
(Northampton, Mass., 1798)

10 **Anthony Philip Heinrich**
THE DAWNING OF MUSIC IN KENTUCKY
Or the Pleasures of Harmony in the Solitudes
of Nature (Opera Prima)
THE WESTERN MINSTREL (Opera Seconda)
(Philadelphia, 1820)

11 **John Bray and James Nelson Barker**
THE INDIAN PRINCESS
Or, La Belle Sauvage, on Operatic
Melo-Drame in Three Acts
(Philadelphia, 1808)

12 **Stephen Foster**
HOUSEHOLD SONGS (1844-1864)

13 **Stephen Foster**
THE SOCIAL ORCHESTRA FOR FLUTE
OR VIOLIN
A Collection of Popular Melodies Arranged
As Solos, Duets, Trios and Quartets
(New York, 1854)

14 **Stephen Foster**
MINSTREL-SHOW SONGS
(New York and Baltimore, 1845-1863)

15 **Lowell Mason**
THE BOSTON HANDEL AND HAYDN SOCIETY
COLLECTION OF CHURCH MUSIC
(Boston, 1822)

16 **George Chadwick**
A FLOWER CYCLE and TOLD IN THE GATE
Twenty-four songs to poems by Arlo Bates
(New York and Boston, 1896-1897)

17 **Simon Pease Cheney**
AMERICAN SINGING BOOK*
(Boston, 1879)

18 **Edward Riley, comp.**
RILEY'S FLUTE MELODIES
(New York, 1816, 1820)

19 **Henry Clay Work**
SONGS
(New York, 1884)

20 **William Billings**
THE PSALM-SINGER'S AMUSEMENT
(Boston, 1781)

21 **Benjamin Carr**
MUSICAL MISCELLANY IN
OCCASIONAL NUMBERS
(Philadelphia and Baltimore, 1812-1825)

22 **Jeremiah Ingalls**
THE CHRISTIAN HARMONY
(Exeter, N.H.)

23 **THE STOUGHTON MUSICAL SOCIETY'S**
CENTENNIAL COLLECTION OF
SACRED MUSIC
(Boston, 1878)

24 **Arthur Foote**
SUITE IN E MAJOR, op. 63 and
SERENADE IN E MAJOR, op. 25
(Boston, Leipzig and New York, 1909)

25 **George F. Bristow**
RIP VAN WINKLE
(New York, 1882)

26 **Arthur Foote**
QUINTET FOR PIANO AND STRINGS
IN A MINOR, op. 38
(Boston, 1898)

27 **John Knowles Paine**
COMPLETE PIANO MUSIC
(Boston, 1864-1889)